T0065643

POTATO JOKES

The Author.

The Illustrator.

PAUL McMAHON

CATHERINE SIRACUSA

POTATO JOKES

BY

PAUL McMAHON

Illustrated by
Catherine Siracusa

LONG SHADOW BOOKS
PUBLISHED BY POCKET BOOKS NEW YORK

Another *Original* publication of LONG SHADOW BOOKS

 A Long Shadow Book published by
POCKET BOOKS, A Division of Simon & Schuster, Inc.
1230 Avenue of the Americas, New York, N.Y. 10020

Text copyright © 1984 by Paul McMahon
Illustrations copyright ©1984 by Catherine Siracusa

Produced by Cognoscenti Books

ISBN 978-0-671-54280-1

First Long Shadow Books printing December, 1984

10 9 8 7 6 5 4 3 2 1

LONG SHADOW BOOKS and colophon are
trademarks of Simon & Schuster, Inc.

Printed in the U.S.A.

ACKNOWLEDGMENTS

I would like to thank the following people for their generous contributions, encouragement and/or just plain patience in assisting the process of this book's coming into being: Catherine Siracusa, Marshall Hambro, Dominick Prezioso, Ed Canavan, Mark Valenza, Suzanne Joelson, Allan McCollum, Marty Asher, Joe Freedman, Laura Ross, Diane Potts, Sherrie Levine, Judy Henry, Jane Leventhal, Louise Gikow and many others at Henson Associates, Mark Saltzman, Katie Dobbs, David Granger and especially Nancy Chunn, whose illness brought about the extremely depressing situation for which POTATO JOKES were an antidote.

POTATO JOKES

What do you call a flirtatious potato?

A croquette.

What's the croquettes' latest hairstyle?

The crinkle cut.

What is casual dress for a croquette?

Mix 'n' mash.

What kind of makeup do croquettes wear?

Pancake.

What do you call a male chauvinist potato?

A masher.

What does a masher say to a cute croquette?

"I got eyes for you, baby."

What do they call the inland waterways of Potatoland?

The Root Canals.

What kind of potatoes catch their own food?

Fishin' chips.

Why do potatoes vacation on the French Riviera?

They like to see the French fry.

What do they do there?

Nothing, they just sit and bake. They can't stay out too long, though. . . . They peel easily.

What is the potatoes' favorite T.V. show?

Mash. Although some prefer CHIPS. Their favorite mini-series was Roots.

What do they drink while they watch?

Spudweiser.

What do russets, new potatoes and Walter Cronkite have in common?

They are all common 'taters.

Why wouldn't the reporter leave the the mashed potatoes alone?

He desperately wanted a scoop.

Why do Valley girls love potatoes?

Because they're "totally tubular."

What's the most popular instrument in the spud marching band?

Potato sax.

What do you call a potato from your neighborhood?

A chip off the old block.

And which potatoes never moved out of the houses they grew up in?

Home fries.

Who was the first potato in outer space?

Spudnik.

Are there potato scientists?

Yes, test tubers.

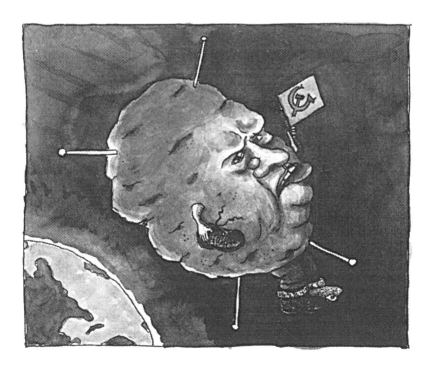

What subject does Professor Potato teach?

Square roots.

Who is the poet laureate of potatoes?

Ogden Mash.

What is a potato's favorite book?

The Good Earth.

Who was the first great spud philosopher?

Platato.

Where do rich potatoes
send their children to
boarding school?

Au Groton Academy.

Where do potatoes go to reproduce?

> *A spud farm.*

Did you know Popeye was a sweet potato?

> *He was always saying, "I yam what I yam."*

Why are potatoes so afraid of Indians?

They don't want to get scalloped.

What disease claims many potatoes each year?

Tuberculosis.

Why are russets always so depressed?

They know they will always be small potatoes.

Why are potato chips considered stupid?

At parties they always hang around with the dips.

Are mashed potatoes honest?

Well, you have to take everything they say with a grain of salt.

How about baked potatoes?

They're worse! Some of them are really full of chive.

How do the poorest potatoes get by?

On a shoestring.

Do potatoes play poker?

Sure. Haven't you ever heard of seven-card spud?

Why do potatoes make such good friends?

You can count on them when the chips are down.

Who is the potatoes' hero?

The Lone Potato.

What kind of horse does he ride?

A scallion.

What do they say after he rides off into the sunset?

"Who was that mashed man?"

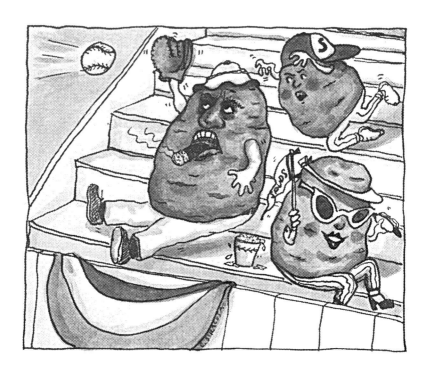

What do you call three potatoes at a baseball game?

Root, Root, Root for the home team.

Are potatoes good at sports?

No, but they are avid spec-taters.

When do the spec-taters cheer?

When the outfielder makes a shoestring catch.

What happens when the potato team is behind?

The french fries play ketchup.

Who is the potatoes' baseball hero?

Babe Root.

What do you call a potato that likes to be beaten?

A Mash-ochist.

What's a mashochist's idea of a good time?

Getting burned at the steak.

Who is the saddest potato in Potatoland?

The blue legume.

What do you call someone who enjoys being introduced to potatoes?

A meetin' potatoes man.

Did you know that Alice B. Toklas' cookbook includes a potato recipe?

Hash Brown-ies. It's the special favorite of Mr. Potato Head.

What do you call Libyan potatoes?

"Pommes de Terrorists."

Where do potatoes race their cars?

The Indianapolis Spudway.

What holiday is sacred to all potatoes?

Mash Wednesday.

Potatoes must be very religious.

*Yes, many of them
become friars. Their
religious leaders are the
Deep Fat Friar and the
Chip Monk.*

Who was the most influential potato theologist?

Martin Tuber.

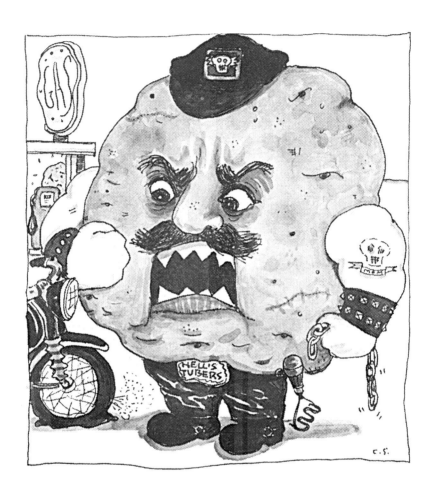

What do you say to an angry 300-pound baked potato?

Anything, just butter him up.

Why can't you insult a baked potato?

They have very thick skins.

What happens when potatoes get really mad?

They get steamed.

And what do they say when they want revenge?

An eye for an eye. And another eye for another eye. And another eye for another eye. . . .

What annual event would no potato dare to miss?

The Mashed Ball.

What do the ladies wear?

Ruffles.

Who rules over the kingdom of french fries?

The Duke of Oil.

What did he title his autobiography?

Lord of the Fries.

Do french fries stay out late at night?

No. Oily to bed, oily to rise.

Why do potatoes dislike Christmas?

They hate to hear that "hoe, hoe, hoe."

Why does every bill pass in the potato legislature?

The _eyes_ always have it.

Why did the potato cross the road?

He saw a fork up ahead.

Did you know that potatoes don't pay any taxes?

They have a totally underground economy.

What kind of potato rents more than one room in a hotel?

A suite potato.

What's a potato's favorite love song?

"Peelings."

What song sets romantic potato couples to dancing?

"I Only Have Eyes for You."

Did you know that
Shakespeare wrote a
play about a sweet potato?

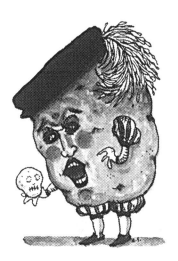

Yamlet. In fact,
Shakespeare loved
potatoes. That's why he
always wrote in i-yam-bic
pentameter.

And what recent Broadway play dealt with
religious potatoes?

Mash Appeal.

What Tennessee Williams play deals with spuds?

Sweet Potato of Youth.

What is the potatoes' favorite highway?

Root 66. They like to cruise along it in their Mash Ramblers.

Did you know you can get arrested for growing too many potatoes?

It's called "exceeding the spud limit."

What's the best way to handle a hot potato?

Butterfingers.

What do potato children play on?

Tater-totters.

What is the french fries' favorite movie?

Grease.

What are potato horror movies called?

"Pommes Frights."

Who is the potatoes' favorite child star?

'Tato O'Neal.

What kind of potatoes roam freely across the African sub-continent?

Gnu potatoes.

Do monkeys like potatoes?

Only potato chimps.

What did the potatoes say to their wives and mothers when they went off to war?

Keep the home fries burning.

What was the national anthem of the Third Potato Reich?

" Deutschland Tuber Alles."
It was sung to honor
their dictater.

What is the war cry of old veteran potatoes?

"Remember the Maine
potatoes!"

What did the drill sergeant say at potato boot-camp?

"Forward, starch!"

What is the country music capital of Potatoland?

Mashville.

What is their favorite song?

"Tennessee Spud."

Who was Dashiell
Hammett's favorite potato?

Sam Spud.

How can you tell when a mashed potato has
committed a crime?

When it is on the lamb.

What crimes are potatoes most often accused of?

Assault and buttery.

What's the best way to murder a potato?

Smother it in onions.

Where are potatoes buried?

Gravy yards.

What did the judge say when sentencing a convicted potato?

"You'll fry for this!"

What did the potato villain say when he was caught and put in the oven?

"Curses, foiled again."

Printed in the United States
By Bookmasters

.